Unweaving the Web

Beginning to Think
Theologically About the Internet

David Clough

Tutor in Ethics and Systematic Theology, Cranmer Hall, Durham

GROVE BOOKS LIMITED
RIDLEY HALL RD CAMBRIDGE CB3 9HU

Contents

Acknowledgments

I am grateful to fellow members of the Society for the Study of Christian Ethics for comments on an earlier paper on this topic, and to students at Cranmer Hall for sceptical and helpful feedback on previous attempts to set out the relationship between theology and technology. Members of the Grove Ethics group also gave me stimulus for further thinking. Particular thanks are due to Dave Leal and Robert Song who commented in detail on full versions of this booklet.

The Cover Illustration is by Peter Ashton

First Impression October 2002
ISSN 1470-854X
ISBN 1 85174 512 2

Introduction 1

There can be few technological changes that have disseminated themselves as rapidly as the Internet.

It was negligible as a phenomenon as recently as ten years ago; now it has over 500 million users. In its infancy, it allowed users only a facility for exchanging text messages; now images, music, video and computer software are readily exchanged, making the Internet an increasingly significant source of information, entertainment, and means of providing services such as retail and banking. The emergence of this technology continues to provoke a wide range of responses. On one hand, there are the exuberant enthusiasts, who see 'cyberspace' as a new frontier promising freedom, democracy, knowledge, adventure and requiring the reinvention of all human social and political structures.[1] On the other, there are those who fear the Internet as giving unrestricted opportunities for pornographers, paedophiles, and drug traffickers, and leading to a future in which all human interaction is reduced to bits and bytes.

This booklet aims to provide some signposts to help orient our thinking in the midst of the change the Internet is bringing, and the extravagant hopes and fears expressed for it. The Internet is young, which should make us shy of precise ethical judgments regarding its legitimacy or use. Yet the scope and impact of this technology is such that it would be irresponsible not to begin reflecting on the meaning of this change in how we order our common life. One part of this reflection is to identify which aspects of the Internet are truly novel and therefore require new responses, and I have structured what follows with this question in mind. The first section describes the Internet and situates the Internet in relation to other technology and thinking about it. The following sections discuss how the Internet affects our understanding of place, time, and personhood. The final section offers suggestions for how we should move forward in increasing our understanding of this technology and shaping our use of it.

Some fear the Internet as leading to a future in which all human interaction is reduced to bits and bytes

2

A New Beginning?

To think clearly about what is new about the Internet and worth noting, we need to escape from the overblown claims that it represents either the end of civilization or its only hope.

One way of doing this is to recall the statements of contemporaries about other, earlier new technologies:

> It will bring everything into harmonious co-operation... triumphing over space and time...to subdue prejudice and to unite every part of our land in rapid and friendly communication.
>
> [It will] give us universally high standards of living, new and amusing kinds of jobs, leisure, freedom and an end to drudgery, congestion, noise, smoke, and filth.

These were predictions of what, respectively, steam power and electricity would enable.[2] My point here is not that new technologies do not change things; both steam power and electricity had far reaching significance for the societies that adopted them. Rather, we should note that those who stand at the threshold of large scale developments should take the hopes and fears they have for them with a pinch of salt. For example, email does alter how we communicate with one another, whom we communicate with and what we say to them, but it does not make us unrecognizably different individuals and communities from those who were once restricted to meetings, letters, phone calls and faxes. We do well to reflect on the novel features of what the Internet brings having freed ourselves from the grand visions of the prophets of the great dawn of humankind or its final dusk.

What is the Internet?

With this sense of proportion, we can turn to describing the technology. The Internet is a global network of computer networks. Local networks belonging to universities, businesses, government departments, schools, and other organizations are linked together so that any computer connected to any of the networks can communicate with any other computer, irrespective of where it is physically located. As long as an email message or web page request is addressed correctly, the Internet servers will find the destination computer whether it is in the next-door office or on another continent. The ability to contact any computer from any other on the Internet is one of the key features that makes the Internet useful and interesting, although for security reasons barriers called 'firewalls' are now widely used by local network administrators to try to prevent outside users from interfering maliciously with the computers on their network.

A second notable feature of the structure of the Internet is that there are multiple paths from one point on the network to another. If one server along the path my message would usually take is not working, the servers around it can send the message around the blockage to reach its destination. This is significant because it makes the Internet difficult to control. Since the Internet has no central server, there is nowhere on the network from which you can see all the information being exchanged, and consequently communication on the Internet is fundamentally unregulated. The UK government, for example, could shut down a server located in the UK that was hosting material considered indecent under UK law. If this server was relocated to the Cayman Islands, however, it would be very difficult indeed to prevent the new server being accessible from the UK as easily as the previous one had been, without also blocking a great deal of traffic that was unobjectionable but travelling along the same routes.

The size, immediacy, uncontrollability, and interactivity of the Internet differentiates it from other technologies

The third structural feature of the Internet worth noting is its size. In May 1982 there were 825 computers hosting information on the Internet; in January 1992 there were 727,000 ; in January of 2002, there were over 150 million. These hosts were serving 37 million websites.[3] In February 2000 there were 281 million users; as of early 2002, 400 million or close to 1 in 10 of the world's population had regular access to the Internet, and the proportion is growing rapidly.[4] The Internet is a significant phenomenon by any measure.

Email and the World-Wide Web are two examples of the kinds of information that can be represented and transmitted across the Internet, but there are many others. As access speeds increase for many users, the Internet becomes a more attractive means of exchanging audio and video files. The combination of this flexibility with the size, immediacy, uncontrollability, and interactivity of the Internet differentiates it from other technologies such as the postal service, telephone, and broadcast and print media. A further notable difference from broadcasting or print publishing is that the Internet allows individuals to publish information with relatively cheap equipment and with knowledge that can be picked up in an afternoon.

What is Technology?

Having gained this perspective on what the Internet is and what makes it unique, it is helpful to put consideration of this technology in the context of the wider theological discussion of technology. In the first place, technology has often been seen as fulfilment of the command in Genesis to multiply and subdue the earth (Gen 1.28). Our technical ability and our ability to reshape our environment to suit us better is taken to be part of what differentiates us from other animals. The tunnels of moles and even the dams of beavers seem tiny efforts in comparison to technical feats such as the Pyramids or the high rise towers that dominate every modern city. The work of Karl Rahner exemplifies this celebration of human technological power. Rahner takes radical freedom to be a fundamental human characteristic, and sees the outworking of this in the way human beings are able to 'stand over *this* world as its lord' through rationality, science and technology. Indeed, Rahner also claims that the self-actualization that gave rise to this possibility is itself a product of Christianity.[5] Karl Barth also affirms proper human creativity in reshaping the world around us,[6] but he is concerned that modern technology is also a way in which human lust for power manifests itself:

> The technical mastery which goes beyond what is vitally necessary, which at bottom has meaning and purpose in itself, and which, in order to exist and augment itself must always evoke new and doubtful needs, inevitably becomes the monster which in many ways we now see it to be, so that finally and ridiculously it is little more than a technique of disorder and destruction, of war and annihilation.[7]

Nuclear weapons were part of Barth's concerns here, which reminds us of the close linkage between the military-industrial complex and the development of many new technologies. His perception, however, that technology may become a monster that dominates us rather than a tool serving our needs has much wider application, and links to the most thoroughgoing theological critique of technology, that of Jacques Ellul.

In a conversation towards the end of his life, Ellul was asked to summarize the main thrust of his work on technology:

> I would say that I have tried to show how technology is developing completely independently of any human control. Carried away in some Promethean dream modern man has always thought he could harness Nature, whereas what is happening is that he is building an artificial universe for himself where he is increasingly being constrained. He thought he would achieve his goal by using technology, but he has ended up its slave. The means have become the goals and necessity a virtue.[8]

In his major work on technology, *The Technological Society*, Ellul defines technique broadly as 'the *totality of methods rationally arrived at and having absolute efficiency* (for a given stage of development) in *every* field of human activity.'[9] While he believes technology began with the machine, he considers the problem as much wider; technique is rational conscious activity dominated by the rational choice of the most efficient means of those available. Machines are the pure expression of this quest for efficiency, but technique is applicable to any activity where efficiency is identified as the central goal.[10]

Using this definition, Ellul disagrees with Rahner that technology should be associated with Christianity and suggests that Christianity has been unsympathetic to technology. He believes that:

- the Emperor Julian was justified in accusing the Christians of ruining the industry of the Roman Empire;
- society at the height of Christian influence between the 10th and 14th centuries was dominated by custom, rather than rationality;
- the technical impetus of Western civilization came from the East; and that subsequent rapid technical development in the West took place in a world that had already withdrawn from dominant Christian influence.

Christian condemnation of luxury and money restricted economic activity and diminished its importance in relation to less worldly goals, Ellul observes, and Christians constantly questioned whether profitable and efficient changes were right and just.[11]

The critiques of Barth and Ellul are a significant challenge to the virtually unquestioned current view that technology is a tool we wield to make life more pleasant for us. There are many debates concerning whether this or that technology—electronic tagging of criminals or cloning of embryos—is a good thing, but science fiction seems the only arena where larger questions are pressed. Mary Shelley's *Frankenstein*, Stanley Kubrick's Hal in *2001: A Space Odyssey*, or the Wachowski brothers' vision in *The Matrix* of a world in which human beings are grown and harvested for fuel by machines, each point towards a world in which the technology that enthrals us has become a monster that enslaves us.[12] The crucial point is that if Barth and Ellul are right these stories are not predictions of the future, but pictures of a current reality. It would be easy to recognize a technological monster if it was approaching us, the size of a house with its laser guns blazing. Their claim is that we are slaves to technology even as we believe we are its master, which, if true, is much more frightening.[13]

The technology that enthrals us has become a monster that enslaves us

The issue of whether or not technology has escaped our control is given an ironic twist by feminist critiques of technology that question the aim of controlling our environment in the first place. Perhaps this longing for control is a specifically male concern, driven by the difficulty men have in their relationship with nature. Simone de Beauvoir is the classic exponent of this relationship:

> Man seeks in woman the Other as Nature and as his fellow-being. But we know what ambivalent feelings Nature inspires in man. He exploits her, but she crushes him; he is born of her and dies in her; she is the source of his being and the realm that he subjugates to his will; Nature is a vein of gross material in which the soul is imprisoned, and she is the supreme reality; she is contingence and Idea, the finite and the whole; she is what opposes the Spirit, and the Spirit itself. Now ally, now enemy, she appears as the dark chaos from whence life wells up, as this life itself, and as the over-yonder toward which life tends. Woman sums up Nature as Mother, Wife, and Idea; these forms now mingle and now conflict, and each of them wears a double visage.[14]

Sally Gearhart has defined technology as 'the conscious and systematic manipulation of one's environment for the purpose of reducing one's dependence on environmental factors for survival.'[15] Technology is thus seen as the essence of the exploitation of nature to which de Beauvoir refers, and it is unsurprising that technological culture has become identified with masculinity. In her discussion of the masculinity of technology, Judy Wajcman narrates the competitive and compulsive work of the group of men involved on the development of the first nuclear weapon in Los Alamos and their response to the dropping of the bomb on Hiroshima. Richard Feynman recounts 'The only reaction I remember was a very considerable elation and excitement…I was involved in this happy thing, drinking and drunk, sitting on the bonnet of a jeep and playing drums, excitement running all over Los Alamos at the same time as the people were dying and struggling in Hiroshima.'[16] Feminists and others disagree, as Wajcman notes, about how far this nexus of men, technology, and weapons reflects essential differences between the sexes, or how far it is a cultural construct. What is clear is that gender is an inescapable factor in reflecting on technology.

At the end of this section we are left with a key question of theological discernment: whether the Internet is an example of how technology privileges efficiency of means over all other considerations. The following sections on place, time, and personhood in relation to the Internet will inform my response to this question, which comes to a focus in the final section of the booklet.

A New Place?   3

In Thomas More's Utopia, *first published in 1516, Raphael Hythloday tells of a wonderful land he has visited where everything is perfectly ordered.*

There is no greed, because each household can take all it needs from a common store. This store always has plenty for everyone, because everyone in Utopia works hard to contribute to what is necessary for communal life and does not waste time in producing what is superfluous. The Utopians wear simple clothes, and have no regard for precious metals or jewels, making their chamber pots from gold to remind them of its worthlessness and giving diamonds and rubies to young children as playthings. There is virtually no crime, because both the penalties for it and the rewards for living virtuously are great. As Hythloday's narrative progresses, however, the reader becomes more and more disconcerted by the cost of this smooth running— authoritarian social control, euthanasia for the non-productive, capital punishment for those who commit adultery twice, the waging of war by paying mercenaries of other nations in preference to risking the lives of the Utopians. More distances himself from Hythloday's enthusiasm by the names he uses. 'Utopia' means 'no place' though it sounds like 'Eutopia' ('good place') and this is the sense in which 'Utopia' is used today. Hythloday means 'peddler of nonsense.'[17]

Cyberspace too is a 'no place' that is often said to be a 'good place,' and yet also has dystopian aspects

Utopia is a helpful point of comparison when faced with references to 'cyberspace,' the environment we are supposed to enter when we request web pages or contribute to online discussions. For this too is a 'no place' that is often said to be a 'good place,' and yet, as we have already noted, it also has dystopian aspects. Cyberspace seems to be beyond conventional categorizations; geographical location means nothing on this worldwide network, so where can events such as online discussion be said to 'take place'? We might say that the same confusion applies to a telephone conference call, but the Internet is both a more immersive experience and is always there even when we are not, and together these make metaphors of space more apposite. Web users often speak of 'visiting' websites, when they ask servers to send data to their web browsers—another spatial metaphor. The Internet is also in competition with geographical space. As I write in July 2002 a journalist is on trial in Zimbabwe for breaking that country's media laws in an article published on a newspaper's website hosted in the UK.[18] Zimbabwe would not claim jurisdiction over printed publications in the UK, but the website can be viewed by citizens of Zimbabwe and this has persuaded prosecutors that its laws apply. It is more or less clear *when* the article was published—when it first appeared on the newspaper's website. But *where* was it published? At the location of the computer used to send the article to the web server? At the location of the web server used to host the pages? At the address of the offices of the newspaper responsible for the website? The fact that the answer to this question is unclear demonstrates that the relationship between geographical space and cyberspace is problematic.

It has the feel of a frontier land, where the rules are not clear

I have already made reference to another problem of jurisdiction, where servers hosting pornographic sites that contravene one nation's laws can be sited in countries without such laws. A different example of the ability of the Internet to subvert authority is the way that Radio Kosovo was able to continue broadcasting on the Internet throughout the Kosovo war, allowing people across the world to hear the Kosovo perspective on the conflict. Some hope that the Internet may become even more threatening to nations; 'cyberlibertarian' activists prophesy that with encrypted communication on the Internet, authorities will be unable to regulate economic transactions between their citizens, resulting in loss of taxation and the eventual collapse of the nation state. While such scenarios are unlikely, it is also unlikely that the Internet will ever be able to be fully regulated. Again, as I write, a group of 'hackers' has made a plausible claim to be developing computer software that will enable completely anonymous and untraceable communication on the Internet.

Patrolling the Global Frontier

If cyberspace is a place, it is a place very different from most locations in the 'real' world. There are some things in common with this other world: you can meet people, be entertained, informed, educated. With the recent explosion in electronic commerce, you can also shop in a bewildering multiplicity of places. Perhaps the most striking difference is that cyberspace has the feel of a frontier land, where there is a great deal to excite interest, but where the rules are not completely clear, and criminal activity can thrive alongside everyday congress because there is no authority with the power to enforce the law. You do not know to whom you are talking in some parts of this place, such as the chat rooms, because the locals here prefer to keep their identities hidden from one another.

Not surprisingly, authorities have made attempts to regulate the Internet. In 1995 both houses of the US government passed the Communications Decency Act, which aimed to make indecent material on the Internet illegal. It was badly drafted, and many groups were concerned that it would prohibit much more than the pornography that was its ostensible aim. There was a widespread protest by those hosting websites and by web users, and a case brought to the US Supreme Court resulted in the law being struck down in 1997. A similar battle has been waged about encryption technology on the Internet. 'Strong' encryption makes it almost impossible to discover what the content of the message transmitted is if you do not have the encryption key. For several years, the US attempted to restrict the export of this technology. But this policy was clearly unsustainable. Web browsers needed to incorporate the encryption and were freely downloadable from the Internet. The companies supplying web browsers went through the motions of conformity with government policy by asking users where they lived; they could only download the software with strong encryption if they claimed to live in the US. It was not hard to realize that this would not be a successful method of preventing export of the technology. Security forces then tried to secure legislation that would give them a 'back door' into the encryption format, which would enable them to read encrypted messages when necessary. There were many objections to this, both from those who objected to the security forces having this power, and from those concerned that other groups would learn the key and would be able to intercept communications, and no 'back door' was created.[19]

For those trying to keep a watch on illegal activity this global frontier land represents a very real challenge

As we saw in the first section, the structure of the Internet makes it resistant to control. With the added factor of encryption in communication, regulating what information is exchanged on the Internet looks impossible. This will not affect most users of the Internet individually; they are statistically unlikely to be victims of crime in cyberspace. For those trying to keep a watch on illegal activity, however, this global frontier land represents a very real challenge.

'Global' is often used as a descriptor for the Internet, as in the previous sentence, but it is worth pausing to examine the accuracy of this term.[20] As the table below shows, the 'no place' of cyberspace is more in some places than others:

Region	Internet Users (millions)	Percentage of World Internet Users	Percentage of World Population
Africa	4.2	0.8	13.3
Asia/Pacific	157.5	28.9	58.0
Europe	171.4	31.5	11.8
Middle East	4.7	0.9	3.1
Canada & USA	181.2	33.3	5.1
Latin America	25.3	4.6	8.6
World Total	544.2		

Table showing number and percentage of Internet users by region. [21]

Comparing the percentage of Internet users with the percentage of world population for each region makes clear the disparity in access to the Internet. Africa has 16 times fewer Internet users than if Internet access were equally dispersed across the world; Canada and USA have over 6 times more users than the world average. Clearly, this disparity reflects the disparity in wealth and infrastructure development between richer and poorer countries. The figures mask the distribution of Internet within countries, but it is a safe assumption that the wealthy in each nation have disproportionate access over the poor. It is crucial in our reflections on the Internet to remember that for all its size, as of mid 2002 only 9% of the world population have access to the Internet, and this is to a close approximation the richest 9%. On this measure the Internet looks like a valuable resource for a small elite to communicate and engage in commerce amongst themselves, rather than a technological means to democracy and egalitarianism, as it is sometimes portrayed. [22]

Only 9% of the world population have access to the Internet, and this is to a close approximation the richest 9%

The Internet is a phenomenon in flux, and it may be that access becomes much wider in the next decade. In the first quarter of 2002, for example, China overtook Japan to become the nation with the second largest number of Internet users (57 million) after the US (166 million). China's figure was well over double the figure for the first quarter of 2001. [23] There is little doubt that poorer nations want more access to the Internet; in addition to the possibilities of communication, the Internet promises relatively cheap access to resources that would be prohibitively expensive to provide by conventional means, such as books and journals. The key issue for these countries is finding the funding to provide computers and the communications infrastructure in situations where there are insufficient resources for much more basic needs.[24]

A Place of Holiness?

The relationships between geographical space and cyberspace traced in this section resonate with theological themes that would bear further reflection than there is space for in this booklet.[25] It would seem, for example, that the idea of being at once dwellers in geographical spaces and belonging to a community in a place that cannot be located in geographical space would not be an unfamiliar one to the Augustine of *City of God*, where Christians are at once members of earthly cities and the heavenly city. There are links between the 'no place/good place/bad place' of Utopia and the theological doctrine of heaven and hell, which might also be fruitful in reflection on the concept of cyberspace. In most religions, a strong link is made between the sacred and particular places; there are places to worship, places to which pilgrimages are made. It is an open question whether there are locations in cyberspace that may be religiously significant in the same way. While a great number of religious groups have set out their stands on the web, I have not come across places in cyberspace that communicate sacredness in the way that a stone circle, a mosque, a synagogue, or a cathedral may,[26] though this may be because of limitations of the current technology that can be overcome as more immersive virtual reality interfaces become more common. There are certainly unholy places, where greed is exploited and resources squandered through electronic commerce, where racial hatred is peddled or child pornography traded. Many would claim, however, that their online experiences of community are far from profane and it would surely be premature to conclude that places in cyberspace cannot participate in holiness.[27] Given the difficulty of regulating the Internet because of its structure, size, and encryption technologies, together with its current status as a network for the rich elite, the question I am left with at the end of this section is whether cyberspace can become a place in which human beings can thrive.[28] Whether cyberspace can be a human place is a parallel question to the question Ellul presses of whether technology is our tool or our master, and I will return to it in the final section.

> *It would surely be premature to conclude that places in cyberspace cannot participate in holiness*

4   A New Time?

On the 23rd of October 1998 the watch manufacturer Swatch launched 'Internet Time.'

Under this system, the headquarters of Swatch in Biel, Switzerland, is taken as a meridian for time units that divide each day into 1000 'Swatch.beats.' This new time is necessary in the new space of cyberspace, according to Swatch:

> Today's world requires a new way of thinking about time.
>
> Swatch has reinvented time with—INTERNET TIME.
>
> Today's lifestyle which demands simultaneous communication with different parts of the world via phones, Internet, email, video-conferencing, and a host of other tools requires a truly revolutionary way of looking at and managing time. Hence, a completely new global concept of time that eliminates time zones and geographical differences was urgently needed. Introducing INTERNET TIME, an innovative, new unit of time, measured in units called '.beats' which allows for:
>
> - No Time Zones
> - No Geographical Borders
> - More Freedom...
>
> Cyberspace has no seasons. The virtual world is absent of night and day. Internet Time is not driven by the sun's position, it is driven by yours—your location in space and time...
>
> Internet Time is absolute time for everybody. Now is now and the same time for all people and places. Later is the same subsequent period for everybody. The numbers are the same for all...[29]

The rhetoric here is fascinating: the corporate branding of 'absolute' time promises equality ('same for all') individual empowerment (a time driven by 'your location in space and time') and more freedom. The metric division of the day recalls the attempted changes to the calendar following the French Revolution, though Swatch seems to have learned from this and makes no comment on 7 day weeks, 28–31 day months, or 12 month, 365–366 day years.

Apart from the frightening science-fiction scenario of a large corporation attempting to take control of time itself, we can smile at the ludicrousness of a new time system that in fact solves none of the problems it claims to. If I am contacting someone in Japan, the time in Swatch.beats does not help me know whether they are likely to be awake.

Unsurprisingly, Swatch Internet Time seems to have won few converts, but I note it here because it illustrates a broader change in attitudes to time in which the Internet has had an important role. While Internet Time has done away with the 24 hours in a day, this perspective on time has much in common with the '24/7' culture that promises goods and services 24 hours a day, 7 days a week. The Internet is not the only force driving the change to '24/7'—supermarket opening hours and customer service phone lines are other examples—but Swatch is right that the Internet makes geographical time zones less relevant, and therefore the concept of the 'working day' is less clear. If you are a UK company marketing to international customers on the Internet, you cannot afford to have no staff available until 9am, when most of Europe will have been at work for an hour or two, or to close the office at 5pm, when New Yorkers are working until 10 or later, and Californians until 1am. Moreover, there is a strong expectation among users that the Internet is 'always on.' So even UK banking customers would be shocked if they were unable to check their current account balances at 2am. In this 24/7 culture the 10,080 indistinguishable minutes of the week succeed one another as monotonously as the Swatch.beats that tick our lives away.

The internet is not the only force driving the change to '24/7'

Ellul would be the first to recognize the efficiency of running commercial operations 24/7. Even those supermarkets not open all night need their suppliers to be, so that fresh goods from great distances can be ready on the shelves. It would be highly inefficient to produce, transport, and market goods only during the relevant working day of each country in the supply chain, and market forces ensure there are economic penalties to being inefficient. This has led to 1 in 5 men and 1 in 10 women working night shifts in the European Union.[30] But Ellul's critique provokes the question of whether this efficient arrangement is the best for the humans who are made part of these systems. Many studies have shown, for example, that shift workers have lower life expectancy than those who work normal hours, and it is clear that quality of life is also affected in the ability of shift workers to participate in family and social life.[31] It is hard to doubt, therefore, that this is a

Is this efficient arrangement the best for the humans who are made part of these systems?

case of efficiency being valued more highly than those things that make for good human life, and the force of Ellul's image of humans enslaved to the technology they have created is difficult to avoid.[32]

Judaic tradition provides the strongest resource for critique of the 24/7 culture. Following the pattern of God's work of creation, the nation of Israel began thinking of time in seven day weeks, six days of which were for work, and the seventh, the Sabbath, for rest:

> Remember the sabbath day, and keep it holy. Six days you shall labour and do all your work. But the seventh day is a sabbath to the LORD your God; you shall not do any work—you, your son or daughter, your male or female slave, your livestock, or the alien resident in your towns. For in six days the LORD made heaven and earth, the sea, and all that is in them, but rested the seventh day; therefore the LORD blessed the seventh day and consecrated it. (Exodus 20.8–11)

The generosity of the Sabbath law is clear, here; not only members of the house of Israel, but slaves, animals, and resident aliens are to be given rest on the Sabbath. Keeping the Sabbath has the two-fold purpose of obedience to God in remembering God's work of creation, and recognizing the need of God's creatures for regular times of rest.

The early church was quick to adopt this pattern, though chose to keep the first day of the week as its holy day in remembrance of the day Christ was raised from the dead. Christian tradition has retained the two-fold significance of the Sabbath following Jesus' teaching that 'the Sabbath was made for human beings, not human beings for the Sabbath' (Mk 2.27). In his Large Catechism, Luther emphasized the human element, stating that we keep holy days 'first of all for bodily causes and necessities, which nature teaches and requires; for the common people, man-servants and maid-servants, who have been attending to their work and trade the whole week, that for a day they may retire in order to rest and be refreshed.' The concern for slaves, servants, and workers evident in the Hebrew Bible and the Christian tradition led to the alliance of UK churches and trades unions in the various campaigns to restrict activities on Sunday, though the efficiency imperative of the 24/7 culture seems to have been finally more powerful.

The Sabbath is a reminder that the world does not depend on human activity

The Sabbath is the gracious divine interruption of human affairs with the reminder that the world does not depend on human activity. The rhythm it introduces indicates the divine origin of creation and makes time human.

The balance of work and rest echoes other chronological rhythms of night and day, and of the seasons. These rhythms are intrinsic to a human experience of time; they are what permit liberation from time as the tyranny of one minute, or Swatch.beat, after another.[33]

There is no law of necessity requiring that a large multi-national computer network should change the way we think about time. We could use the Internet in a way that respected the rhythms of our local environment. The technology might even help us do it: email messages can be waiting for their recipient to answer when they get to work, whereas the telephone is reliant on two people communicating at the same time; e-commerce sites allow orders to be taken in the absence of salespersons. There is precedent for using technology to order time in creative ways; the first all-mechanical clocks may well have been developed by monasteries that needed to know when to pray. Yet the way we in fact have adapted to this technology weakens our grasp of the rhythms in time that sustain us, and there seems a structural bias in the technology that encourages us towards the 'always on' 24/7 culture. If Ellul is not to be proved right, we will have to demonstrate that we can make this technology work to human hours, rather than dying early in an attempt to adapt ourselves to Swatch.beat Internet time.

The way we have adapted to this technology weakens our grasp of the rhythms that sustain us

5 A New Person?

If you have never tried Inter-Relay Chat (IRC), on the Internet, try it sometime.

At any given moment, thousands of conversations are taking place on an astonishing variety of topics with participants from many parts of the world. Choose a name to call yourself, and a 'chat room' from those available, and you find yourself part of an interchange with others that you know nothing about apart from the messages they exchange. Many find it a liberating experience; for the first time, they find a place where people are not reacting to their spotty face, or bust size, or height, or stutter, or deafness, or black skin, or wheelchair, or age, or gender, or sexual orientation, but just on what they say. Frank conversations can take place that would be impossible or highly unlikely in face to face encounter, and a sense of fellow feeling, trust, and community can develop with individuals that you may meet regularly when you return to the chat room. Beyond the freedom of establishing relationships that are independent of your physical features, the anonymity of chat rooms give you the chance to experiment with aspects of your identity. How about taking a position on a political or ethical issue that is opposite from your own, for fun, or to see what it feels like? Since no one will ever know who you really are, there is nothing to stop you. Have you ever wondered how it would feel to be treated as a member of the opposite sex? Then tell them you are a woman, or a man, and see what happens.

Many find Internet chat a liberating experience

The degree of anonymity possible in the chat room is an unprecedented phenomenon unique to the Internet in which people can interact with one another as never before.

There are clear ethical issues in relation to deception in Internet chat rooms. A recent *Coronation Street* plot showed a young teenage girl lured to a rendezvous with a much older man in the belief that the person she had met in a chat room was a boy her own age. Clearly, children need to be warned of these dangers. Yet while the Internet provides a new environment for the activity of paedophiles and other criminals, the issues here are not unique to the Internet. The technology of the car led in a similar way to warnings to children not to accept lifts from strangers.[34]

The experience of participating in Inter-Relay Chat provokes much larger questions about what it means to be a person. If I can interact meaningfully with others independently of my physicality, does this mean my body is less important to me than it previously seemed? There are currently many stories of couples meeting via the Internet and then agreeing to meet in person, but what if some of my most significant relationships were conducted entirely online? If I can experiment with my identity when I interact in this way, I could take on different persona in different contexts. Does this give the lie to the idea that my identity is singular and holistic? Does it make me realize that all I ever do, online or offline, is to take on social roles in relationship with others? If in a chat room I can playfully tell others things about me that are untrue, and this deception has no consequences, does this indicate that I should take a more playful attitude to deception in my life offline?

Other online environments in the future may push some of these questions further. Imagine, for example, choosing not just a name, but a three-dimensional image to represent yourself in a fully immersive virtual reality experience. You could choose to be the supermodel physique you have always dreamed of, or to be a dolphin, or an eagle, and use this body to explore whatever virtual environment you chose, interacting with others through the virtual identities that they had selected.[35]

Identity and Responsibility

The novel environments provided by the Internet in chat rooms and virtual reality experiences will reveal new insights about what it means to be human. It would be strange if it were otherwise; new contexts reflect different aspects of ourselves back for us to see. Landing on the moon impresses us with both human capability, and also human insignificance in the extraordinary size of the universe. Cyberspace will give us its own new perspectives on our humanity. Christian theology must be open to what can be learned from these insights. Yet alongside this openness, I think it important to set down at least one marker relating to an aspect of personhood that cannot be abandoned in the exploration of cyberspace. Anonymity is fun to play with in particular contexts—masked balls and blind man's bluff are real world examples of this—but not being anonymous, being known by others, is fundamental to being responsible. It is this aspect of the self as responsible that we cannot let go of in our quest for the new insights cyberspace may bring.

Being known is fundamental to being responsible

The relationship between identity and responsibility is clear in daily life. If I cannot be identified, then I cannot be held accountable for my actions. And if I succeed in remaining anonymous I cannot be asked to answer for what I have done, because no one knows to whom to address the question. Identity and responsibility are clearly linked in the Jewish tradition, too. In the Hebrew Bible, Israel is not any old nation, but the nation chosen by God:

> Do not fear, for I have redeemed you;
> I have called you by name, you are mine. (Is 43.1)

For Israel, being chosen and known by God is to be responsible before God in covenant relationship. It is therefore unsurprising to find the Jewish philosopher Emmanuel Levinas emphasize responsibility as an inescapable aspect of selfhood. For Levinas, I can only understand myself in relationship to the other person who confronts me as utterly unknowable and incomprehensible. He rejects modern accounts of personhood that begin with freedom, because he claims that my encounter with the other resists me and destroys my freedom. Always already the other has held me hostage and placed me under infinite responsibility. I cannot go beyond or behind this having been obliged. I cannot attempt to contain the other, or my responsibility, by stepping outside of our relationship and seeing this other and myself as instances of some universal truth. Any such attempt transforms the other into the same, the known and comprehended. The other elects me to this responsibility, which is uniquely and irreplaceably mine.[36]

The Face of the Other

Crucially for our task here, Levinas says that it is the face of the other that represents and bears this otherness to me.[37] The face is the antithesis of anonymity, as wanted posters and identity parades make clear. Reflecting on the problem of anonymity as getting away with crime focussed on the agent's anonymity, but attending to Levinas shows that the identity of the *other* is just as important in order to be responsible. Part of what is attractive about anonymity is that we do not have to respect the otherness of the individuals we interact with. If we confront an individual with knowledge of their identity, we cannot avoid acknowledging their otherness and the ways we cannot comprehend them. Anonymous individuals, on the other hand, give no indication of their difference, and tempt us to reduce their otherness to sameness.

Why is a person facing a firing squad often blindfolded? It may enable him or her to avoid flinching, but it also helps those shooting forget that they are killing a fellow human being. If I cannot see the face of the person I meet online, and I know nothing about them, there is no basis for my recognition of all the ways they are other than me and incomprehensible to me. Without experience of their difference from me, I am likely to assume that I can categorize them in multiple ways, that they are the same as the other faceless individuals I meet online. I am also less likely to feel responsible to them. I might find it fun to deceive the anonymous user 'cyber3' into believing that I held various politically absurd views, but once I know that this is Jonathan Robbins, who is 32, lives in Liverpool and works as a delivery driver for a local haulage firm, I am likely to feel more obligation to be truthful in my communication with him. If Levinas is right, as I believe, the promise I alluded to above that anonymity means an escape from prejudice will prove illusory, because it is only engaging with the other in full appreciation of their difference that will lead to mutual respect. 'Face' serves as a metaphor for Levinas here. It is not that I could never be aware of the otherness of the other who confronts me if I cannot see their physical face—his thought does not deny the possibility of authentic confrontation with another via telephone, or online. It is *anonymity* online that precludes this possibility.

Responsibility always pertains even in anonymous communication

The Christian rite of baptism supports this account of the relationship between identity and responsibility. At baptism, new members are given a Christian name in front of the assembled congregation. They make vows and are made responsible for keeping them (or others are made responsible on their behalf). But just as in Levinas's thought it is encountering the other that makes me responsible for them, so after this naming the congregation are asked to take responsibility for supporting the new church member in their Christian life. Thus it is the bestowing of this identity that calls for responsibility both on the part of the individual, and on the part of those who are called to recognize this new identity.

Legitimate Anonymity

None of this is to say that anonymous chat rooms are illegitimate; I have already indicated that I consider them to offer unique new possibilities of human interaction and through these and other computer-mediated forms of interaction we may learn a great deal. In fact, of course, responsibility always pertains even in anonymous communication. I might flippantly advocate the violent overthrow of the UK government and be taken seriously by one of those present, whether or not they know who I am, or, in an example featured on the radio yesterday, young women might be heavily influenced by others anonymously recommending anorexia as a route to looking like a supermodel. Most contributors to chat rooms recognize the responsibility they have and are often active in policing the contributions of others with this in mind as well as developing a tradition of 'netiquette' specifying appropriate behaviour in cyberspace. The early development of the Internet, before its massive commercialization, was characterized by an astonishing generosity among users, and this spirit of aid and cooperation is still evident in many places in cyberspace. My purpose here has not been to criticize the practice of anonymous chat on the Internet, but to begin a response to the questions this anonymous interaction poses for our understandings of personhood. In particular I suggest that reflection on the thought of Levinas makes clear that one of the attractions of anonymity—both in terms of keeping our identities hidden and of not knowing the identities of others—is that we believe we can behave irresponsibly towards others. Whatever we learn from the Internet about personhood, it cannot be that this irresponsibility is a legitimate part of being human.[38]

A New Task?   6

In the preceding sections, I have attempted to identify the features of the Internet that are novel and theologically challenging, and to begin the task of a theological response through considering how these features affect the way we think about place, time, and identity.

In this final section my aim is to point forward to some of the consequences of these reflections for how we should think about and make use of the Internet.

One temptation when confronted with a new technology that has problematic aspects is to reject it. This is rarely a viable option, and is not in relation to the Internet. Roman roads must have been recognized to have many disadvantages when they were first built, such as the rapid spread of disease and making it easier for enemies to mount an attack from a distance. Refusing to use the roads, however, would not have been a useful response to such worries, and certainly the early Christian church took full advantage of them. The Internet does bring serious concerns with it. As well as the larger concerns I have identified, I have referred in passing to pornography, which may well be the largest economic activity in cyberspace, and to the ease with which criminals may be able to communicate without risk of interception.

But there is no route back to a less connected planet, and even if there were, too much would be lost on the way. The Internet is here to stay, and not using it will soon be at least as great a handicap to life in the 21st century as not using the postal system or the telephone.

There is no route back to a less connected planet, and even if there were, too much would be lost on the way

We must, then, make use of the Internet, but this necessity is also a permission which we can embrace and enjoy. I have not had space in the preceding reflections to detail the many riches to be found on the Internet. My own background includes time spent designing web sites and programming for web servers, and my colleagues will testify of my enthusiasm for what the Internet makes possible. From world newspapers on the morning of their publication, to the full text of Thomas Aquinas' *Summa Theologica*, to a live scoreboard for all the courts at Wimbledon, to recipes for chocolate brownies, to Multi-User Dungeon gaming—the Internet offers an astonishing range of information and possibilities for interaction with other users.[39]

The Drive of Technology

Given that we may use this technology, the new task facing us is how to use the Internet responsibly and how to shape its development. Beyond any of the specific ethical issues that arise in connection with the Internet, the fundamental question is how the Internet may be made a technology that *enables* human living, rather than threatening it. Ellul's concern was that through technology we are trying to harness nature by constructing an artificial world that turns out to constrain, limit, and dominate us, and I noted the close relationship between this and the feminist critique of a masculine pursuit of technology in reckless abandon of its consequences. The perspectives of de Beauvoir and Wajcman are helpful in moving one step beyond the critiques of Barth and Ellul I have noted here, because they remind us that technology is not some abstract force that has its own life, but is the activity of concrete human beings—male ones, for the most part. Behind the idol of efficiency, the worship of which Ellul so dramatically unmasks, there are people who are enriched by our worship. In the case of the 24/7 culture I discussed this is clear; there is no mysterious Internet-related demon driving us to work through the night to feed it, and thereby shorten our lives. It is to the economic advantage of company directors, managers, and shareholders—a category to which any of us who are part of a pension scheme belong—to make employees work inhuman hours. It would be overly reductionistic to claim that the imperative towards technological development can be explained entirely by consideration of economic—or gender—power relationships; there is a fascination with the creative power of work of our hands and minds that escapes such an analysis. We should be in no doubt, however, that this fascination is very frequently co-opted to serve the domination of other human beings and the wider created order.

How can the Internet be made a technology that enables human living, rather than threatening it

Let us use it in awareness that it has the potential to dominate rather than serve our live

Let us, therefore, use the Internet to amuse and inform ourselves, facilitate human relationships, make life easier, and allow us to learn about others and ourselves in new social contexts. But let us use it in awareness that this technology has the potential to dominate rather than serve our lives and those of others. The promise of the Internet to connect the world is indeed a grand new beginning, far more significant than the growth of the telephone network. Cyberspace is a new and exciting place that justifies elements of grand utopian visions, though it is currently only the playground of the richest 9% of the world's population. Yet it also threatens human living; it tempts us to an unholy and inhuman view of time that treats human beings as machine parts, and tempts us to think there are places in cyberspace where we can hide from one another and escape from the responsibility that the identity of the other places upon us.

The Internet is in its infancy. With or without us it will grow through adolescence into adulthood. What it becomes depends on whether its users are able with wisdom to embrace its gifts and steer it carefully from the many paths down which it could go astray.

Notes

1   See, for example, Esther Dyson *et al*, *Cyberspace and the American Dream: A Magna Carta for the Knowledge Age*, 1.2, August 22 1994, Progress and Freedom Foundation, available at: http://pff.org:80/position.html.

2   James W Carey, 'The Mythos of the Electronic Revolution,' *Communication as Culture: Essays on Media and Society* (New York: Routledge, 1992) pp 120, 130, cited by Grant Kester in Grant H Kester, 'Access Denied: Information Policy and the Limits of Liberalism,' *Ethics, Information and Technology*, Richard N Stichler and Robert Hauptmann (eds) (Jefferson, North Carolina: McFarland and Co, 1998) p 208.

3   Source: Robert Zakon, 'Hobbes' Internet Timeline,' version 5.6, 1st April, 2002 (URL: http://www.zakon.org/robert/internet/timeline, visited 19th July, 2002).

4   Source: NUA Internet Surveys, URL: http://www.nua.ie/surveys/how_many_online/world.html, visited 15th July, 2002. Estimating the number of Internet users is not straightforward, but other groups give similar figures. See section 2 for a regional breakdown of these figures.

5   Karl Rahner, 'The Experiment with Man' in *Theological Investigations* Vol IX (London: Darton, Longman, and Todd, 1974) p 214, italics in original.

6   See, for example, Karl Barth, *Church Dogmatics*, Vol III/4, G W Bromiley and T F Torrance (eds) (Edinburgh: T & T Clark, 1961) pp 470–1.

7   Barth, *Church Dogmatics*, Vol III/4, p 395.

8   Partrick Troude-Chastenet, *Jacques Ellul on Religion, Technology and Politics: Conversations with Patrick Troude-Chastenet*, Joan Mendès France (trans) (Atlanta, Georgia: Scholars Press, 1998) p 119.

9   Jacques Ellul, *The Technological Society*, John Wilkinson (trans) (London: Jonathan Cape, 1965) p xxxii, italics in original.

10 Ellul, *The Technological Society*, pp 1–22.

11 Ellul, *The Technological Society*, pp 32–7.

12 *2001: A Space Odyssey*, Stanley Kubrick (dir), 1968; *The Matrix*, Larry and Andy Wachowski (dirs), 1999.

13 Stephen Monsma makes the more limited claim that technology should not be considered neutral. See Stephen Monsma et al, *Responsible Technology: A Christian Perspective* (Grand Rapids, Michigan: Eerdmans, 1986).

14 Simone de Beauvoir, *The Second Sex* (New York: Modern Library, 1968) p 144, cited in Patrocinio Schweickart, 'What If…Science and Technology in Feminist Utopias,' in Joan Rothschild (ed), *Machina Ex Dea: Feminist Perspectives on Technology* (New York: Pergamon Press, 1983) p 202.

15 Sally M Gearhart, 'An End to Technology: A Modest Proposal,' in Rothschild, *Machina Ex Dea*, p 171.

16 Cited in Judy Wajcman, *Feminism Confronts Technology* (Pennsylvania: Pennsylvania State University Press, 1991) p 139.

17 See Clarence Miller's Introduction in Thomas More, *Utopia* (New Haven and London: Yale University Press, 2001).

18 'Guardian Reporter's Trial Resumes in Harare,' *The Guardian*, July 12th, 2002.

19 See Diana Saco, *Cybering Democracy* (Minneapolis and London: University of Minnesota Press, 2002) pp 157–180.

20 John Weckert draws attention to this question in 'What is New or Unique about Internet Activities' in Duncan Langford, *Internet Ethics* (Houndmills, Basingstoke, Hampshire: St Martins Press, 2000) p 48.

21 Internet user estimates from NUA Internet Surveys, URL: http://www.nua.ie/surveys/how_many_online, visited 15th July, 2002. World population estimates from the Population Reference Bureau 2001 World Population Datasheet (URL: http://www.prb.org/Content/NavigationMenu/Other_reports/2000–2002/sheet1.html, visited 15th July, 2002). The population figures are for mid 2001, but the error resulting from the slight mismatch between this and the date of the Internet user figures is insignificant for the magnitude of the trends I am assessing here.

22 For an examination of the claim that the Internet is a democratic technology, see Deborah G Johnson, 'Democratic Values and the Internet,' in Langford, *Internet Ethics*, pp 181–9.

23 Robyn Greenspan, 'China Pulls Ahead of Japan,' article on CyberAtlas (URL: http://cyberatlas.internet.com/big_picture/geographics/article/0,,5911_1013841,00.html, visited 16th July, 2002).

24 The UNESCO Observatory on the Information Society provides links to regional initiatives to develop Internet access (URL: http://www.unesco.org/webworld/observatory, visited 16th July, 2002)

25 For a starting point on place as a theological theme, see Karl Barth, *Church Dogmatics* Vol III/4, pp 285–323, and Stephen Radley, *Place: Church and Mission* (Grove Pastoral booklet P 70). The final chapter of Graham Ward, *Cities of Good* (London and New York: Routledge, 2000) pp 225–260, is an insightful exploration of the relationship between theology, geographical space, and cyberspace in 21st century Britain.

26 To take your own view of this, visit the First Church of Cyberspace (URL: http://www.godweb.org), or one of the UK denominational home pages: *eg* Church of England, URL: http://cofe.epinet.co.uk; Methodist Church, URL: http://www.methodist.org.uk; Roman Catholic Church, URL: http:// www.catholic-ew.org.uk.

27 For a discussion of the prospects for religious community online, see Heidi Campbell, 'Finding God Online,' in Heidi Campbell and Jolyon Mitchell (eds), *Interactions: Theology Meets Film, TV and the Internet* (Edinburgh: Centre for Theology and Public Issues, 1999).

28 For empirical studies on how human beings interact with the Internet, see the

journal *CyberPsychology and Behavior*, Mary Ann Liebert Inc, Larchmont, NY.

29 Swatch Group, Internet Time Brochure, 1998 (URL: http://swatch.com/alu_beat/internet_time_brochure.pdf, visited 16th July, 2002).

30 National Institute for Working Life, Sweden, 'The 24h Society: Work Hours, Health and Safety,' 18th June, 2000 (URL: http://www.niwl.se/wl2000/work-shops/workshop26/article_en.asp, visited 17th July, 2002).

31 See, for example, J Takula, International Labour Office Geneva, 'Introductory Report: Decent Work, Safe Work,' paper presented at the XVIth World Congress on Safety and Health at Work, Vienna, 27th May 2002, available at URL: http://www.ilo.org/public/english/protection/safework/wdcongrs/index.htm, visited 17th July, 2002.

32 The alternative market-driven explanation is that this incidence of shift work arises because companies are able to pay sufficient premium to individuals in recognition of efficiency gains from shift working that they freely choose to contract for the work in spite of the long term consequences to their health. Given the limited choice of employment open to most individuals, I do not consider this plausible. For a wider discussion of the consequences of a global economy on human living, see Nicholas Boyle, *Who Are We Now? Christian Humanism and the Global Market from Hegel to Heaney* (Edinburgh: T & T Clark, 1998).

33 See Karl Barth, *Church Dogmatics* Vol III/4, 47–72, for further discussion of the Sabbath.

34 Jeroen van den Hoven provides a useful guide to categorizing moral issues according to whether the Internet is necessary and/or sufficient for them to occur in 'The Internet and Varieties of Wrongdoing,' in Langford, *Internet Ethics*, 132–134.

35 See Graham Houston, *Virtual Morality: Christian Ethics in the Computer Age* (Leicester: Apollos, 1998) for discussion of the ethical aspects of virtual reality technology.

36 The aspects of Levinas's thought I describe here are found in 'Philosophy and the Idea of the Infinite,' reprinted in Adrian Perperzak, *To the Other* (Purdue University Press 1993) pp 88–119; *Totality and Infinity*, Alphonso Lingis (trans) (Martinus Nijhoff, 1979); *Otherwise then Being or Beyond Essence*, Alphonso Lingis (trans) (Martinus Nijhoff, 1981). Peperzak's introduction to Levinas' work in *To the Other* is helpful in orienting the reader new to Levinas.

37 David Ford has explored the complexities of the relationship between identity and faces, and this area of Levinas's thought, in *Self and Salvation* (Cambridge: Cambridge University Press, 1999) see especially ch 1.

38 For consideration of other aspects of the way the Internet affects our ideas about personhood, see David Pullinger, *Information Technology and Cyberspace: Extra-connected Living* (London: DLT, 2001).

39 For a considered affirmation of the possibilities of the Internet, see Church of England Board for Social Responsibility, *Cybernauts Awake! Ethical and Spiritual Implications of Computers, Information Technology and the Internet* (London: Church House Publishing, 1999).